Rejection

Biblical Truth Simply Explained

Baptism in the Holy Spirit
Jack Hayford

Biblical Meditation
Campbell McAlpine

Blessings and Curses
Derek Prince

Deliverance
Bishop Graham Dow

Forgiveness
John Arnott

The Holy Spirit
Dr. Bob Gordon

Prayer
Joyce Huggett

Rejection
Steve Hepden

Spiritual Protection
Lance Lambert

The Trinity
Jack Hayford

Trust
Tom Marshall

Worship
Jack Hayford

Rejection

Steve Hepden

Chosen Books

A Division of Baker Book House Co
Grand Rapids, Michigan 49516

Published in the USA in 2003 by Chosen Books
a division of Baker Book House Company
P.O. Box 6287, Grand Rapids, MI 49516-6287
www.bakerbooks.com

Originally published by Sovereign World Limited of Tonbridge, Kent, England

Printed in the United States of America

Library of Congress Cataloging-in-Publication Data
Hepden, Steve.
    Rejection / Steve Hepden.
        p. cm. — (Biblical truth simply explained)
    Originally published: Tonbridge : Sovereign World, 1992.
    ISBN 0-8007-9347-1 (pbk.)
    1. Rejection (Psychology)—Religious aspects—Christianity.
    2. Consolation. 3. Rejection (Psychology)—Biblical teaching.
    4. Consolation—Biblical teaching. I. Title. II. Series.

BV4905.3.H47 2003
248.8'6—dc21
                                                            2003055055

To my wife, Chris, without whom it would never have happened, who in the midst of her own suffering let me go to fulfill God's purposes.

To my daughters, Joanna and Zoe, who have been so caring and patient with their dad.

To the many people over the years who have given themselves to be counseled by me.

Also to my friends in leadership who have trusted and released me to pray for many hurt and afflicted people.

Notes for study leaders

The issue of rejection affects many people. The personal way in which it is addressed in this book is likely to bring up strong feelings in people, perhaps including you as leader. Do not be surprised if tears surface as some wounds are reopened, particularly when answering certain questions.

As a leader, you will need to balance the needs of individuals with those of the whole group. It is best to model an accepting attitude toward emotional responses. At the same time, it is wise not to get sidetracked into devoting too much time to any one person in the group.

Some group members may be quick to rush in with advice or counsel for someone who is obviously hurting. That may not be the most helpful response, however, and may in fact be a way of defending themselves against their own painful memories and feelings!

The focus of this study is the healing power of the cross for anyone suffering from rejection. Our hope is that healing will come as people think and pray through the issues on their own and in the group setting. However, some may well benefit from more counseling and prayer outside of the group, through the wider Church.

Encourage group members to read the chapters prior to each meeting and think about the issues in advance. It is usually good to review the content of the chapter at the meeting, however, so that those who have not managed to "do their homework" will not feel embarrassed. Five study questions at the end of each chapter will stimulate thought and encourage people to consider how any of these issues may affect them personally.

May God bless you as you study this material yourself and lead others in doing so.

Contents

1	Understanding Rejection	11
2	Why Rejection Is a Problem	17
3	The Spiritual Source of Rejection	22
4	The Physical Roots of Rejection	28
5	The Fruit of Rejection	36
6	Jesus and Rejection	44
7	Dealing with Rejection	49
8	Moving On from Rejection	55
	Appendix: Family History Questionnaire	58

1

Understanding Rejection

The little girl was standing all alone in the railway station of the big city. Her parents had been fighting with each other and had finally gone their separate ways. Neither of them was prepared to take their three-year-old daughter, so they left her alone at the station.

Ann had become an orphan, although both of her parents were alive. She was taken into care and, until her teenage years, stayed in a well-known orphanage. Can you imagine what went on in that child's heart?

There was nothing subtle about her rejection—it was open and obvious. She was not wanted, she was not loved, she was thrown away like rubbish.

Ann grew up with a desperate hunger to be loved and cared for. As a teenager, she grasped for anything that would satisfy her inner longing for acceptance. Her boyfriend would creep up the fire escape into the orphanage at night, sleep with her and then get out quickly before the matron did her early morning visits.

Many say that children are too young to really understand and be affected by rejection. Yet our experience tells otherwise.

Tony had six sisters, five of them from different fathers, some of them of different races. He had little idea of which man was his father. Imagine the confusion, the rejection and the hurt that came through this disturbed family setting. Tony was emotionally crippled by insecurity and self-rejection. He was naturally sensitive but was unable to handle deep relationships.

Years later, Ann and Tony each became Christians. They both joined the same church fellowship in their hometown. After a very special meeting where the Holy Spirit moved in great power, we prayed for Ann and Tony. As the issue of rejection came up for Tony, Ann began to react severely. The same happened as we prayed for Ann—Tony was deeply affected. It took time, but it was amazing to see the Holy Spirit begin to deliver them both at the same time!

Tony and Ann fell in love with each other and got married. They now have a daughter whom they love dearly. There is no rejection—it has gone. They are more secure than ever before in their lives. Out of their childhood hurts, wounds and bondages of rejection, they have found the love of God and acceptance in each other.

What is rejection?

Rejection is very often linked to childhood injuries. It can come from a significant person's refusal to acknowledge or accept us. It can result from being forsaken or abandoned, giving a sense of being discarded as useless, unsatisfactory or worthless. Feelings of rejection often arise from not being loved as we are, but feeling that we need to constantly act a part.

We all need and crave love—it is the way God made us. In an atmosphere of love, acceptance and approval, we can grow into a sense of security and well-being.

The existence of rejection does not necessarily mean that there is no love at all in the home. Often parents are caring, but because they themselves did not receive all that they needed in childhood, they are unable to express affection, touch or the spoken word that builds up or affirms. If these things are absent, feelings of rejection will flood in uninvited to fill the void.

When people feel unloved or unwanted, these feelings can be coupled with a sense of worthlessness. This leads to feelings of inadequacy, inferiority and insecurity: "I hate myself. Everyone is better than I am or does things better than I do."

Often the hurting person will suffer a loss of identity. He or she may be desperately asking, "Who am I? Where am I going? What is my role?"

For many, guilt enters the picture. This can lead to strong self-rejection and a tendency to continually speak negative words to oneself. "Maybe God is punishing me. I am a bad person. I can never change." Many destructive thoughts can be entertained.

Deep wounds in the inward self are often revealed outwardly by unhealthy behavioral patterns and defensive attitudes. The person who feels rejected may have great difficulty accepting love, spoken affirmation or physical expressions of affection. Self-protective barriers go up because of the fear of unbearable further rejection. No one is allowed close.

Such wounds require emotional healing through prayer and counseling, healing that is available through the Lord Jesus.

Identity and image

God has made us as individuals with unique personalities. We are all different, and we are all important in God's plan. In the beginning God said, "Let us make man in our image, in our likeness" (Genesis 1:26). As human beings, we reflect God's likeness. We were created to represent the reality of who He is.

Self-image is the way we see ourselves. It is a map, drawn according to our self-beliefs, that we consult concerning ourselves. When we become Christians, the Holy Spirit makes us alive to God. If our self-image is unhealthy (the map is wrong), there will be a conflict between the way we see ourselves and the way we know God sees us.

Our self-image can be affected by different sources. In our early years we totally depend on the reactions around us to help us arrive at an understanding of who we are. A newborn baby is completely open and impressionable. The growing child's perception of life is filtered through the words, attitudes and behavior of its parents and other significant figures. As we looked through this childhood mirror, what reflection did we see? The distortions from that time are never forgotten.

From childhood we also pick up many of the world's ideas. These can affect the way we see ourselves, positively or negatively. Our individual makeup can also influence the way we feel and respond to particular circumstances. Moreover, Satan is the accuser, the one who whispers words of condemnation and guilt. He is the father of lies and tries to stop us from believing that God actually accepts us.

When Jesus was asked what the greatest commandment was, He summed it up very clearly: " 'Love the Lord your God with all your heart and with all your soul and with all your mind.' This is the first and greatest commandment. And the second is like it: 'Love your neighbor as yourself' " (Matthew 22:36–39). How can we love God and our neighbor if we cannot even accept or love ourselves?

We have a built-in need for recognition and acceptance. Jesus fulfilled this and enabled us to have peace with God and with ourselves. Yet we may have been conditioned by our environment to believe that we can only gain acceptance by behaving in a certain way.

When we fear rejection, we tend to wear "masks" so that we do not have to reveal the real person underneath. We behave differently depending on who we are with. We hide our true feelings, constructing an unreal image to impress others. If we have experienced rejection, we think our identity is in what we *do*. God tells us that our identity is in what we *are!*

God sent His Son—the very stamp of God's nature and being—to restore and redeem us. Yet rejection often has such a deep root in us that we cannot accept this. We still feel worthless, useless, inferior and inadequate.

Proverbs 27:19 says, "As water reflects a face, so a man's heart reflects the man." Rejection can make us think and act in a way that is consistent with the distorted feelings inside but is dishonoring to God.

Can demons be a source of rejection?

Rejection violates the very character and heart of a person. It quickly bruises the spirit. My experience of counseling shows clearly that demonic powers will enter through such wounds and feed on them. There are certain types of evil spirits specifically related to rejection, often entering through some sort of trauma.

We cannot be sentimental: Evil spirits do not respect vulnerable people, and they can cause damage even from the womb. Evil spirits must have an open door to enter a person, but rejection can become that door to affliction and oppression.

When demons become attached to emotional wounds, they cause bondage. People may therefore need both the healing of their wounds and the breaking of demonic bondages. We need to discern, asking the Holy Spirit for guidance.

In some cases, rejection can have ancestral roots. It is quite possible for children to inherit wounds and demonic influences linked to rejection. The Lord told Moses that He punishes children and grandchildren for the sin of the parents (Exodus 34:7). Many times in counseling I have found the source of rejection in past generations, living or dead.

It is common for Christians to believe they cannot be affected by demons. Yet when we became Christians, did we permanently stop sinning or getting ill? Alas, no! Similarly, we are taught to possess the land and overcome in the name of Jesus. But we sometimes fail because of our human weakness and sin.

In some cases, demonic powers came in before the person was born again. It is actually the power of the Holy Spirit within and the Christian's choice to grow in God that has exposed the demonic.

It is true that the word demon *possession* is not entirely right, though it is used in some translations. *Possession* means ownership, and Christians have deliberately submitted to the ownership and lordship of Jesus Christ, not any demonic power. A demon cannot invade and indwell a person's spirit if the Holy Spirit is there. But as we have seen, demons can hinder or block Christians in their spiritual life. A better translation is "to have a spirit," or to be "demonized."

Because we are undiscerning, problems often go unrecognized for years. Yet each time there is a trigger event, rejection rears its ugly head.

It has been said that rejection is the greatest undiagnosed, and therefore untreated, illness in the Body of Christ today. If that is true, as I believe it is, what causes rejection, how can we recognize it and how can we deal with it in the Church?

Study questions:

1. How do you respond when you look in a mirror? Do you feel good?
2. Are you important in God's plan? Do you feel needed and of value in the Kingdom?
3. Do people really love you? Do you have a healthy sense of belonging? Are you aware of being wanted, accepted, cared for and enjoyed?
4. Do you feel that you have the ability to get through life? Can you cope competently with situations that arise?
5. Can you move freely as the person God created you to be? Or are you locked up in yourself, feeling condemned and guilty?

2

Why Rejection Is a Problem

Mephibosheth was one of the many rejected people mentioned in the Bible. Second Samuel 4:4 records the childhood event that affected the rest of his life. When he was five years old, the news came that his father (Jonathan) and grandfather (Saul) had been killed in battle. His frightened nurse picked him up to flee, but Mephibosheth fell (or perhaps was dropped), and he became crippled in both feet.

Names in the Old Testament can give insight into the personalities or destinies of the people who possessed them. In Hebrew, Mephibosheth's name means "from the mouth of the shameful thing." He was not only crippled physically at an early age, but was also crippled inside. The death of his father and grandfather caused a great loss. (It is common for children to feel rejected by people who leave them, even by death.)

Mephibosheth was also left with a physical deformity that would isolate him from others and cause feelings of self-rejection, inadequacy and inferiority. His family's defeat meant the loss of his royal inheritance. He grew up to be a physically and emotionally broken man, in a place called Lo Debar, which itself means "barrenness, infertile, no pasture."

I know many modern-day Mephibosheths, affected by roots of rejection, crippled within by shame and living in barren places. Rejection that begins at a very early age often becomes an inseparable part of the person, stunting his or her growth in every way.

We read the sequel to this story in 2 Samuel 9:1–13. Years later King David remembered his covenant of friendship with

17

Jonathan and asked if there was anyone left in that family whom he could help. Ziba, an old servant of Saul, mentioned Mephibosheth, and the king sent for him. When the two men met, David promised to show kindness to Mephibosheth and restore the land of his father and grandfather. From then on, he would eat at the king's table as an honored guest.

Mephibosheth's answer is revealing: "What is your servant, that you should notice a dead dog like me?" (2 Samuel 19:8). His self-denigrating words reflected the sense of worthlessness that he felt inside. Yet the king spoke words of restoration and reconciliation, restoring to Mephibosheth and his offspring their lost inheritance.

We see in this a picture of how our King Jesus desires to bring healing to us. He calls us to sit and eat at His table, and He restores to us what we have lost. Psalm 23:5 expresses it so well: "You prepare a table for me in the presence of my enemies. You anoint my head with oil; my cup overflows."

We want this overflowing cup, and we want God's anointing. But unless we deal with roots of rejection within us, they can prevent us from sitting at the table to commune with God.

Rejection affects the whole person

The story of Mephibosheth shows that rejection is not just a slight and short-lived problem. It is something that can affect us our whole life. It can also affect our entire self—spirit, soul and body.

Spirit
Wounds coming through the circumstances and traumas of life can affect every part of us, even our spirit. Because of this, it is not surprising that so many rejected people have difficulty in their relationship with God.

When God created Adam from the dust of the ground, He breathed His life into him so that Adam became a living being. This breath—or spirit—is the unique gift of God. It is the capacity within us to encounter God, become conscious of Him and experience His presence.

The Bible is very clear that this area of our being can be affected negatively. Proverbs 18:14 says, "A man's spirit sustains him in sickness, but a crushed spirit who can bear?"

The enemy plays a part in oppressing our spirits. Jesus said that the devil comes to steal, kill and destroy (John 10:10). Some people can have a demonic "spirit of rejection" that needs to be overcome by the authority of Christ.

Soul

Rejection will certainly affect our soul. This includes our will, intellect and emotions. The ability to make right decisions and choices about the way we behave can be compromised by our reaction to past rejection. A sense of rejection can also affect our memories and hinder our capacity to think and reason. Finally, it can affect our emotions, either to the extent that we seem to have no feelings or that we cannot control our feelings.

When we are told again and again that we are no good, it alters us on the inside. Our own emotions begin to tell us the same thing, and our outward behavior gives the same message to other people. They can then act as if programmed to reject us! The message of rejection is reinforced again and again.

Body

Some people experience rejection because they have been told constantly that they are ugly or have been made fun of because of physical problems. Many people believe they are the wrong shape—too big, too small, too thin, too fat, too long a nose, etc. Self-rejection, focused on the physical body, can quickly take over. It may well affect our health, our posture and our appearance.

The fact that we live in a media-saturated and image-obsessed society can make us acutely conscious of imperfections in our physical shape and size. Teenagers and young women are particularly subject to this and, consequently, may abuse their bodies in the name of style and beauty. We need to thank God for our bodies. We also need to be responsible in the way we treat them.

Rejection affects all relationships

How can a person who feels totally rejected accept the love of God? It is not easy. They find it difficult even to get close to other people. Feelings of rejection in current relationships often occur with very little apparent cause. It becomes more comfortable to keep the barriers up and refuse to let others in.

Sometimes people cannot give love because they have not received love themselves and they cannot understand it. They cannot receive what they do not recognize, and they cannot give what they do not possess. So rejection grows a little more, in a vicious cycle. In the story of Mephibosheth, we can see that he seemed almost to turn away from David's offer of welcome and support.

Rejection can affect every area of a person's life, deeply wounding the inner personality and spirit. It can begin at any time, although it is most commonly rooted in childhood or even the womb. Although it may not be seen as such in those early years, rejection is like a seed that takes root in a certain kind of soil and perhaps manifests later. A trauma or negative circumstance can trigger and release it, and another layer of rejection will take place.

Is rejection easy to cure?

Basically, no! Rejection causes major problems with multitudes of people, whether they are Christians or not. It is essential that we do not rush to solve a problem too quickly when that person has been hurting for many years.

Rejection is part of the curse on humankind. We need to face it realistically, knowing that discernment, patience, mercy, understanding and authority are all required. Often discipleship or mentoring can be part of the follow-up work.

Without knowledge of the Holy Spirit, we are lost—we must listen to Him and trust Him to lead us.

Study questions:

1. In what ways did Mephibosheth experience rejection?
2. How did those experiences form him as an individual? Were there any ways in which he was liable to perpetuate the pattern of rejection in his family?
3. What aspects of a person can be affected by rejection?
4. In what way does rejection affect relationships?
5. Do any of these issues affect you personally?

3

The Spiritual Source of Rejection

To understand the nature of rejection, we need to look at its origins. Often people are unaware that rejection is the source of their problems, because they only look at the fruit and go no further.

You may be surprised to know that the source of rejection is in the very beginning of humanity, with the original sin of Adam and Eve and their sons Cain and Abel. It seems that rejection has been around as long as human beings!

The core issue here is not roots—which we will look at later—but source. In order for roots to grow, a seed must be planted in a certain kind of ground. It is this ground that is the source of the rejection that plagues us.

The Garden

The Garden of Eden was created by God as a place of harmony and complete relationships. In it Adam and Eve could commune together, communicating freely with each other and with their Maker. They would often hear the sound of God walking in the Garden, and they were at one with Him.

Genesis 1:31 sums it up: "God saw all that he had made, and it was very good." Not just good, but very good! Both the man and the woman were totally affirmed and accepted in their identities and secure in their roles. As they lived in the Garden, they had a true sense of worth and belonging.

It was in this garden that God gave the man and woman a commission that was to last forever. Genesis 1:28 says, "God blessed them and said to them, 'Be fruitful and increase in number; fill the earth and subdue it. Rule over . . . every living creature.'" So from the beginning God told them to be fruitful sexually and to take authority spiritually. This was to be their truest calling and capacity. God gave them everything they needed to live fulfilled and satisfied on this earth.

The enemy

It was in this ideal environment that Satan came to tempt Adam and Eve. He struck at the heart of the issue by challenging their willingness to submit to God. Satan said of the forbidden fruit, "God knows that when you eat of it your eyes will be opened, and you will be like God, knowing good and evil" (Genesis 3:5).

In this one event Satan undermined God's word, gave Adam and Eve false expectations and distorted their image of God and of themselves. They had to make a choice about whether or not they would continue to obey God's commands.

God gave human beings free will, the right and responsibility to make choices. They chose to believe the serpent instead of their Creator. In rebelling against God, Adam and Eve rejected Him.

The curse

Usually when God came into the Garden, there was happy fellowship. But after the man and woman rejected God, they hid in fear and shame. Neither would take responsibility for their sin: The man blamed the woman, and the woman blamed the devil (Genesis 3:11–13).

Yet they were all accountable because they had chosen to turn away from God and disobey Him. Because of this, they lost their spiritual, mental, emotional and physical harmony with each other and with God. Instead of innocence, there was shame; instead of relationship, there was division.

Because of their rejection of God, He ejected Adam and Eve

from the Garden. Their disobedience became a curse to them as they were exiled to a fallen world. They could not return: Death had set in. At that point, rejection took root for them and their offspring, and through them the whole of the human race.

The offspring

After the Fall, Adam and Eve were isolated and damaged. Even the animals and the land seemed to be against them. Into this fallen world their sons Cain and Abel were born.

It seems that something of the rejection of the parents passed to Cain, their firstborn. Throughout Scripture the firstborn has significance: Abel offered the firstborn of his flock to God (Genesis 4:4); firstfruits of the harvest were a special offering to God (Deuteronomy 26:1–4); God calls Israel His firstborn son (Exodus 4:22). Perhaps because Satan was aware of the special nature of the firstborn, he wanted to destroy it right from the beginning.

In any case, there is a generational link with the sins of the parents. The opening that Adam and Eve gave the devil was also a blight on their offspring. It seems unfair, yet Cain still had a choice about sin.

The offerings

Genesis 4:2–5 tells us that Abel kept flocks and Cain worked the soil. They each brought some of the fruits of their labor as an offering to God, but only Abel's was accepted. Hebrews 11:4 tells us, "By faith Abel offered God a better sacrifice than Cain did. By faith he was commended as a righteous man, when God spoke well of his offerings. And by faith he still speaks, even though he is dead."

Abel's offering was by faith—a pure response to God. By contrast, it would seem, Cain's offering was to do with works—to get acceptance and affirmation for himself. Scripture indicates that his motives were impure. First John 3:12

says, "Do not be like Cain, who belonged to the evil one and murdered his brother. And why did he murder him? Because his own actions were evil and his brother's were righteous."

The reaction

Genesis tells us that Cain was very angry and his face was downcast. There was a mixture of resentment and self-pity that led to rebellion. Yet God came in grace and compassion to reason with Cain. He asked why Cain was so angry and upset, and said, "If you do what is right, will you not be accepted?" (Genesis 4:7).

God was giving Cain another opportunity to get it right. Yet Cain wanted it his way, not God's. So often we have to make the choice of responding to God. Obedience will mean acceptance, but disobedience will mean rejection.

The warning

God then gave the critical warning to Cain: "But if you do not do what is right, sin is crouching at your door; it desires to have you, but you must master it" (Genesis 4:7). This is a prophetic warning about what was happening in the spiritual realm—the enemy was lying in wait at his door, ready at any moment to come in.

God was letting Cain know the seriousness of his situation and telling him what choice he had to make. We can never put all the blame on our personal hurts or on the devil: We still have personal responsibility. God said Cain must master, or overcome, the sin lurking inside him. He would not say that unless it was actually possible to overcome, by His grace!

The judgment

Tragically, Cain chose to ignore God's words. He enticed Abel into a field and killed him (Genesis 4:8), releasing all of his hatred and anger onto his own brother. When God asked him what had happened, he lied, saying he did not know, and then asked defiantly, "Am I my brother's keeper?" (Genesis 4:9).

The result was a curse. In rejecting God and His ways, Cain became his own victim and was rejected by God. He became a marked man and was driven to be a restless wanderer throughout the earth.

In Genesis 4:13–14 Cain says to God, "My punishment is more than I can bear." He is filled with anguish, paranoia and fear of persecution and death. "I will be hidden from your presence . . . and whoever finds me will kill me."

This is a very significant picture of rejection. Because rejection is tied up with identity and image, many rejected people never find fulfillment in who they are. They are always driven to look for something more, something they can never find. This restlessness means they can never find satisfaction, continually reinforcing their sense of rejection.

These early passages from Genesis show us the source of rejection. It is clear that rejection has been a curse on humankind from the very first family and that it can be hereditary, passing down through the generations.

It is also clear that Satan and his demonic powers have a significant part to play in rejection. Nevertheless, we have free will to choose good or evil, and we cannot ever absolve ourselves of personal responsibility. Scripture entreats us, "Do not be like Cain" (1 John 3:12), and judges those who have "taken the way of Cain" (Jude 11). It is a serious message to us all.

Study questions:

1. What does the story of Adam and Eve tell us about rejection?
2. How did their rejection of God lead to His rejection of them?
3. Why was Cain particularly vulnerable to the curse of rejection?

4. In what way may your own feelings of rejection lead you to sin against God or others?
5. Is there a way out?

4

The Physical Roots of Rejection

When a seed has been planted and the conditions are right, it is not long before the roots begin to grow. Roots are normally the hidden parts of the plant, yet they are vital to the whole. The roots of a tree anchor and support it and are a source of nourishment. They may be as deep in the ground as the tree is tall—anyone who has tried to dig out the roots of a large tree will understand how difficult and lengthy a job it is.

We cannot disregard the roots of rejection. They are often deep and strong, have developed for many years and need careful and sensitive handling when they become exposed, ready to cut off.

It is fairly straightforward to deal with fruit in a person's life, just as it is easy to pick the fruit off a tree. Yet if the roots are not dealt with, the negative fruit of sin will return again and again and cause frustration. The Lord said of the sin of the Amorites, "I destroyed his fruit above and his roots below" (Amos 2:9). It is vital to identify the roots of rejection so they can be dealt with.

There are many reasons why rejection may come about, and they may affect us at any time, from the beginning of life. From these specific incidents, the roots and fruits of rejection develop.

Conception and pregnancy

Rejection can begin in a wound or demonic oppression before a child is born. The enemy takes advantage of the most

28

vulnerable. Many adults have found the source of their problems in infancy or even earlier.

In *The Secret Life of the Unborn Child*,[1] the authors state, "The unborn child is an aware, reacting human being who from the sixth month on (and perhaps earlier) leads an active emotional life." They add, "The fetus can see hear, experience, taste and, at a primitive level, even learn in *utero*. Most important, he can feel, not with an adult's sophistication, but feel nonetheless."

Verny and Kelly go on to say, "What a child feels and perceives begins shaping his attitudes and expectations about himself. Whether he ultimately sees himself (and hence acts) as an unhappy or sad, aggressive or meek, secure or anxiety-ridden person depends, in part, on the messages he gets about himself in the womb."

Therefore it is clear that a denial of love can affect a child before it is born. The womb is the child's first home. Is it friendly or unfriendly, peaceful or hostile? The child will receive both parents' feelings and thoughts. Their attitude and relationship with the baby before it is born will affect it after it is born.

The following are reasons for rejection before birth:

- Unwanted pregnancy, possibly because of conception too soon after marriage, conception very late in life, too large a family or financial problems

- Illegitimacy (Deuteronomy 23:2 speaks of a curse extending to ten generations. This can be cut off in Jesus' name.)

- Exceptional fear of deformity or fear of childbirth

- Attempted abortion

- Pregnancy through rape, incest, adultery

- Drug- or alcohol-dependent mothers

- Separation or divorce before the baby is born

- Shock or trauma during pregnancy, such as an accident or death of someone close

[1] Thomas Verny and John Kelly, *The Secret Life of the Unborn Child* (New York: Summit, 1981), pp. x–xi.

We can be encouraged by many comforting words in Scripture. God is very concerned about children in the womb. The psalmist puts it very clearly:

> For you created my inmost being;
>   you knit me together in my mother's womb.
> I praise you because I am fearfully and wonderfully made;
>   your works are wonderful,
>   I know that full well.
> My frame was not hidden from you
>   when I was made in the secret place.
> When I was woven together in the depths of the earth,
>   your eyes saw my unformed body.
> All the days ordained for me
>   were written in your book
>   before one of them came to be.
>   Psalm 139:13–16

Birth

It is clear that rejection can stem from the actual birth or events soon afterwards. All these things can be factors:

- Pain and trauma of a long, protracted labor
- Difficult delivery, especially if instruments are used
- Emergency attention after birth requiring separation from the mother
- Congenital deformities
- The mother's death at the time of the baby's birth
- The baby being taken away for adoption
- Feeding problems interfering with mother-baby bonding
- Parents' inability to show affection or give loving touch
- Parents wanting a boy instead of a girl, or vice versa, so that the child takes on guilt for being the "wrong" gender (This can be made worse if the couple is convinced that God told them the baby would be a different sex!)
- The child not being named for a long time after the birth

- A child who was conceived as a "replacement" because an older sibling died
- Parents or doctors being unaware of a second baby in the womb

Early childhood

Rejection can also affect a child as it is growing up. The first few months and years of a child's life are foundational and formative. Children mirror those who are close to them, and their spirits are wide open to receive both positive and negative things.

- Phrases such as "You were a mistake," "We didn't want any children," "We really wanted a boy/girl," "I wish you had never been born" (Proverbs 18:21 says, "The tongue has the power of life and death.")
- Separation too early in life or for too long, even for legitimate reasons
- Children given up for adoption or to foster homes in their early years, even if they are later welcomed into a loving home
- Preferential treatment of one child over another, which may lead to attention seeking and friction between siblings
- Early losses, such as death, divorce or separation
- Physical or mental disabilities, even speech impediments and the like
- Prolonged childhood illness or hospitalization
- Parents arguing or fighting in the family home

School years

Rejection can occur in the very important years up to adulthood. The relationships between parents and children are key to a person's development. How we learn to view ourselves can affect us deeply.

- Cruelty or domination by parents or older siblings
- Lack of affection and physical touch in the family
- Parents persistently ignoring the child
- Serious lack of communication in the family
- Negative comparison with other children in the family or at school
- Being sent to boarding school
- Being humiliated, severely punished or unfairly treated by teachers
- Bullying, exclusion from groups of friends and name-calling
- Constant sickness
- Excessive pressure from parents to succeed in school
- Religious pressure and legalism
- Name-calling, emphasizing personal qualities or physical features
- Speech or learning difficulties, such as stuttering and dyslexia
- Personal beliefs, such as "I'm no good," "I'll never make it," "I'm too fat/thin/tall/short/ugly" or "I want to be someone else"
- Lack of affirmation of a child's developing sexuality in adolescence

Family circumstances

There is much that happens within the family and sometimes in outside circumstances that can cause rejection.

- Poverty or serious financial problems
- Racial abuse

- Long periods of unemployment
- A family member convicted of a crime or imprisoned
- Parents forcing their children into immoral or criminal behavior
- Sexual abuse, inside or outside the family
- Prematurely giving a child adult responsibilities
- A clinically depressed or mentally ill parent
- Alcoholism or other addictions in the family
- Shame or persecution about religious beliefs
- Unfaithfulness, separation or divorce of parents
- Ill-treatment by step-parents
- Premature death of a parent or other family member

Later life

Well into adulthood traumatic incidents can occur that create or highlight rejection issues.

- Guilt over a teenage pregnancy, sexual experience or abortion
- Failed love affairs
- Unwanted singleness
- Infertility
- Being disabled or having a major illness
- Serious problems with children
- Divorce, separation or unfaithfulness of spouse
- Death of a marriage partner or other significant person
- Being evacuated or becoming a refugee in times of war

All of these issues are important and need to be considered sensitively. I would like to comment further on two of them.

▶ *Abuse*

The incidence of abuse is now much more common, or commonly known. Abuse can begin in the earliest years.

Verbal or mental abuse is any form of negative pressure by thoughts or words. Adults as well as children can be easily put down by words. Long silences can also be used manipulatively. Some people are persistently ignored when they talk, and that also is a form of rejection. Remember the power of the tongue for good and evil!

Physical abuse can affect children, marriage partners or unmarried partners. The physical damage is bad enough, but there is also emotional hurt and humiliation that may take a long time to heal. There is a right and a wrong way to discipline children.

Sexual abuse is much more widely recognized than it was previously. The wounding it causes is a ready opening for demonic activity. Because this abuse is surrounded by secrecy, the awareness of abuse is usually suppressed, and its effects are buried deep within the person who has been victimized.

If abuse happens within the family, it engenders especially deep guilt, distrust, hatred and confusion. Children often endure the pain and shame out of loyalty or the fear of reprisals. The violation of their dignity, humanity and sexuality will bring problems in later life, especially in marital relationships. The person will grow up with a sense of defilement and inner conflict.

Abuse means betrayal, and it is always accompanied by feelings of rejection.

▶ *Broken marriages*

Separation or divorce of parents inevitably leads to some form of rejection. The rights and wrongs of the situation are not ultimately the issue. The spoken vows and the sexual act itself create a spiritual bond: As it is often declared at a church wedding, "Whom God has joined, let no one put asunder."

The tearing apart of separation and divorce causes deep wounding to the partners involved and also to the children.

This can be particularly difficult for Christians, especially those in leadership. We need to be aware of the pain and rejection of being cast aside, the sense of worthlessness, as well as the loss of income, home, friends and school. For children it can mean losing the relationship with one, or even both, parents.

Summary

It is clear that traumatic circumstances, and our responses to them, can cause roots of rejection to form that may affect the rest of our lives. It is vital that we understand the emotional, social and spiritual impact of these experiences of rejection so we can face them in the power of the Holy Spirit.

Study questions:
1. Do any of the adverse circumstances listed for the time of conception, pregnancy and birth apply to you?
2. What about early childhood and school years—do any of the things on the list seem to stand out as particularly relevant to your own life story?
3. How about family circumstances and later life?
4. Have you been personally affected by abuse or a broken marriage?
5. What can be done for you or for others who have suffered in any of these areas?

5

The Fruit of Rejection

Fruit can be defined as the product or result of something. When a seed is sown, it will root into the ground, and when it is mature, it will produce a seed-bearing body, usually above ground.

Rejection produces its own distinctive fruit. It is often easy to identify the fruit and deal with it without touching the root, but then the fruit is liable to return. That is why I have first emphasized dealing with the root.

The fruit of rejection may manifest in either outward, visible behaviors or hidden, inward ways. It is important to understand the fruit so that the roots may also be recognized.

In an outward, visible reaction, people can be over-emotional, loudly expressing anger, or be aggressive or over-bearing. Rejected people sometimes defend themselves by attacking others. Because of their fear of being hurt, they put up defensive barriers against access to their own hidden feelings, while at the same time reacting strongly to others.

In an internal, hidden reaction, emotions may be suppressed as with a dam while long-hidden memories are still affecting the person. Rejected people often escape into themselves because it is easier to hide than to cope with reality. There may be a reluctance to communicate honestly, so the real person is not seen.

Whether outward or inward, the response is unconsciously motivated. In other words, people do not know why they react as they do or why they are having problems in everyday life. This will affect their sense of identity and basic role in life.

Three main types of fruit

The harmful fruit of rejection can be grouped into three basic areas. Looking first at these three main areas can help us understand the various reactions or symptoms that are displayed by rejected people.

Rebellion

Rebelliousness is an aggressive reaction to rejection that shows itself as opposition or defiance. When a rejected person reacts this way, anyone who gets in his or her way can be affected. Anger, arrogance or criticism may be openly displayed. These emotions may normally be deeply hidden but will erupt like a volcano when provoked, injuring the person and those around him or her.

There is a definite link between rebellion and witchcraft. Samuel said to Saul, "For rebellion is like the sin of divination, and arrogance like the evil of idolatry. Because you have rejected the word of the LORD, he has rejected you as king" (1 Samuel 15:23). Remember Cain? Often evil spirits are behind rebellion and control, greatly increasing the problem.

Self-rejection

Many people take rejection into their own selves and begin to reject and hurt themselves. This can be through hating themselves, cursing themselves or being physically violent toward their own bodies. This can be terribly destructive and even lead to suicide.

There is a sick self-orientation in this reaction. The roots of rejection keep growing while being fed by self-rejecting thoughts, words and actions. It is not difficult to turn the thoughts of rejection inward, and many of those who do so think of it as less sinful than outwardly directed aggression. Yet when we reject ourselves, we will finally reject the God who made us.

Self-protection

Self-protection is caused by fear of rejection. Fear is always around the corner when rejection affects a person. The fear of additional hurt will create defensive barriers that are hard to dismantle and which create major barriers to relating to others.

Many rejected people ask themselves, "Can I trust anyone? Will I be hurt again?" They close off inner feelings, taking control so that no one can get close enough to cause the same damage. Some people become seemingly emotionless because their defensive barriers are so impregnable.

Different reactions

Because people react differently to rejection according to their personalities, there can be manifestations of any of the main roots. It is not uncommon for all three to be involved. The mind, will and emotions can all be influenced, causing attitude and behavior change.

One man whom I counseled felt unable to respond to God as Father, and his emotions were completely locked up. He had experienced rejection in early childhood that had left a strong reaction of anger and hate (rebellion), deep insecurity, inadequacy and inferiority (self-rejection), as well as criticism and pride, fear of failure and domination (self-protection). The outward expression was anger and hate, while inwardly his deep hurts had blocked off early memories and prevented him from weeping.

These fruits can be demonic. There are actually demons called "rebellion," "self-rejection" and "self-protection," and even simply called "rejection." We need to learn to discern between demons and wounds, and to know when both are present.

One demonic power called the "orphan spirit" is clearly linked to lack of love, care, affectionate touch, security and right discipline in a person's early months or years. Ultimately, a spirit may seek to oppress such a person. He has a sense of being orphaned or abandoned, regardless of whether the parents are actually living, and is resistant to receiving love from others. People affected by this spirit find it hard to respond to the Father heart of God. How can they when they have not received love from their earthly parents?

Control is another issue closely linked with rejection. It is a conscious or unconscious power over another person that manifests as domination, superiority or emotional manipulation. This can be driven by a reaction to past rejection. There is also a link between wrongful control and witchcraft. The Holy Spirit will be grieved by inappropriate domination and manipulation, and strong occult spirits can come in.

Suppression of emotions and memories can also be a form of control related to rejection. The dam that is created is a hard and harsh reaction covering up much hurt. If a spirit of control comes in behind it, a bondage will be created. I have known many people who come to faith afflicted with this kind of control and are unable to release their emotions, worship freely or be open to the moving of the Holy Spirit. It is vital to discern these roots so that they can be released.

A more outward form of control is domination. Rejected people have a fear of further rejection and will try to control a situation or person to make sure this does not happen. They may do this by conditional love—threatening to withdraw love unless a person submits to their control. Because children are very dependent, they are especially vulnerable to wrong forms of control. One example is the "Jezebel" spirit, referred to in Revelation 2:20–22, which involves false teaching or prophecy, sexual immorality and strange religious practices.

Often a child rejected and traumatized in the early years is stunted in his or her emotional growth, and a demonic bondage may also be present. I have met many adults who are, in part, still little boys or little girls and react with inappropriate emotion to certain situations. Of course, the emotions need releasing and healing, while the demonic powers must also be dealt with. Great sensitivity is needed!

Recognizing the fruit of rejection

The fruit of rejection is revealed in different signs and symptoms. If we can be informed about their meaning and relate them to our own personalities, a picture will be built up that will help to identify the roots of rejection.

One example of a character weakness is insecurity—lacking confidence in situations, being unsure or unstable. Linked with other key symptoms, it will highlight the possibility of a root of self-rejection.

I often use the following words as a diagnostic test for people whom I suspect have a root of rejection. Each word is defined to help explain the meaning. I go quickly through the list, asking people to mark themselves honestly on a scale of zero to five according to how closely the word applies to them: Zero would mean the word does not apply at all, and five would mean it very definitely does.

You can go as far back over the years as memory allows. It may help to involve someone close to the person, possibly the spouse, in order to get his or her opinion or confirmation. Remember to be discerning and sensitive to the Holy Spirit. Whether the fruits are fleshly reactions or actually demonic, discipleship will be necessary in follow-up.

As the marks are added up in the word groupings, a particularly high score in one section suggests the presence of that specific root.

Fruit relating to rebellion

- Harshness: severe or rough language
- Hardness: unyielding and impenetrable attitudes
- Unbelief: refusal or inability to believe
- Skepticism: strong doubt or undermining attitude
- Defiance: hostility, resistance, disobedience
- Pride: overly high opinion of own qualities

- Arrogance: feeling of superiority shown in an overbearing attitude
- Stubbornness: unwillingness to give way in situations
- Anger: rage, fits of temper or smoldering anger
- Violence: destructive actions
- Bitterness: deep-rooted resentment and poisoned attitudes
- Addiction: use of drugs or other substances to remove emotional pain
- Occultism: witchcraft, divination, New Age practices, idolatry
- Legalism: exalting law over grace
- Lust: excessive, self-centered desire for power, sex, money, etc.
- Control: domination or manipulation of others
- Aggression: pushy and offensive behavior
- Refusing to receive affection: will not receive comfort from others
- Argumentativeness: given to quarrels and disputes
- Vengefulness: tendency to retaliate verbally or physically

Fruit relating to self-rejection

- Negative self-image: the belief "I am worthless"
- Inferiority: the sense of being lower than everyone else
- Inadequacy: inability to cope with tasks, the words "I can't"
- Sadness: intense unhappiness, depression
- Grief: anguish and feelings of loss
- Shame: feelings of disgrace and humiliation
- Self-accusation: constant sense of guilt or being wrong
- Self-condemnation: sense of needing to be punished, inability to accept praise

- Inability to communicate
- Fear of failure: panic attacks
- Insecurity: lack of confidence
- Disappointment: constant sense of unfulfilled desires
- Loneliness: isolation and pain of being alone
- Hopelessness: despair, sense of "no way out"
- Wrong expectations: inappropriate assumptions
- Seeking to please: need to find favor with everyone
- Anxiety: worry, fretfulness, apprehension
- Infirmity: sickness or physical disability brought on by self-rejection

Fruit relating to self-protection

- Pressure to perform: "I must be competent in order to gain acceptance"
- Pressure to achieve: "I must be successful in everything"
- Striving: trying too hard, strenuous effort that causes inner conflict
- False responsibility: taking on inappropriate burdens
- Restlessness: drivenness, inability to settle or to find contentment
- Competitiveness: "I must be superior to everyone else"
- Independence: "I can do without you. I will do everything myself"
- Self-centeredness: "I'm only interested in myself"
- Self-justification: always seeking to excuse oneself
- Self-righteousness: always right, never wrong in own eyes
- Criticism: constantly finding fault, disapproving and undermining
- Judgmentalism: authoritatively hostile attitudes toward others

- Jealousy: suspicion of others who have what you want
- Envy: intense desire to have what another has
- Self-pity: sulking, constantly sorry for oneself
- Possessiveness: need to hold on to or control others or things
- Perfectionism: excessive need to get everything right
- False gratification: looking for comfort from wrong sources—e.g., food, sex, drinking
- Self-deception: "No one understands me," false beliefs
- Fear of betrayal: unwillingness to trust anyone
- Rejection of others (often in situations when under pressure in relationships)
- Unreality: withdrawal into fantasy world, avoidance of reality
- Shyness: timidity, uneasiness or avoidance of other people

Study questions:

1. What fruits of rejection can you see in yourself that are related to rebellion?
2. What fruits can you see in yourself that are related to self-rejection?
3. What fruits can you see in yourself that are related to self-protection?
4. Is there one area of the fruit of rejection that is most prominent in you personally?
5. What are you going to do about these areas of difficulty?

6

Jesus and Rejection

The key to the healing of rejection lies with Jesus. We need to consider how He identified with rejection from the very beginning of His life through to His death on the cross. It has been said that Jesus was the most rejected person who ever lived. Yet He never let rejection overcome or control Him. He never manifested any of the fruit of rejection, because the roots were never allowed to take hold.

Jesus suffered rejection, but He did so in order to set us free from its grip. John sums up the rejection of Jesus: "He was in the world, and though the world was made through him, the world did not recognize him. He came to that which was his own, but his own did not receive him. Yet to all who received him, to those who believed in his name, he gave the right to become children of God" (John 1:10–12).

Jesus' birth and early life

Luke 1:26–38 describes how Mary (likely as young as sixteen years old) was greatly surprised and troubled by the appearance of an angel announcing that she would give birth to a baby by the Holy Spirit. The problem was that she was pledged to Joseph (Matthew 1:18–20), which under Jewish law was as serious a commitment as marriage. Mary could have been stoned as punishment for unfaithfulness.

In such a society, not much remained secret. Imagine the gossip and the scandalous rumors. Joseph struggled with the news, planning to break the marriage contract because it was not his baby. It took an angel to convince him to marry Mary.

A census in the Roman world meant that the family had to travel to their home town of Bethlehem to register (see Luke 2:1–5). It was at least a three-day journey, very difficult for a pregnant woman. When they arrived at Bethlehem, there was no accommodation for them, though it would seem likely that Joseph had extended family there—why could they not provide a room? Jesus was born in a cave-like stable with domestic animals.

This hardly sounds like the ideal start in life. But more sinister events were to come. King Herod, hearing from the Magi that the Messiah was to be born, wanted to kill Jesus. He ordered a massacre of all the male children of two years old and under. Jesus' family fled to Egypt, where they remained until the ruthless king's death. They then returned to an obscure, poor town called Nazareth, where Joseph set up his carpentry business.

When Jesus was twelve years old, He accompanied His family to the Temple in Jerusalem. A crisis occurred when Jesus was missing for three entire days. His parents finally found Him in the temple with the teachers of the law (see Luke 2:41–50). When Mary asked Jesus why He had treated them in such a way, she was astonished and probably angry. They did not understand His reply: "Didn't you know I had to be in my Father's house?" (Luke 2:49). Their lack of comprehension about His call must have added to the rejection Jesus had to deal with.

Jesus' ministry

Throughout the three-and-a-half years of Jesus' earthly ministry, He experienced much rejection. When crowds began to gather to hear Him, His own family went to take charge of Him, saying that He was out of His mind (Mark 3:21). John tells us that even His own brothers did not believe in Him (John 7:5).

After Jesus spoke in the synagogue, people were so furious that they drove Him out of town, trying to throw Him over a cliff (Luke 4:28–30). Matthew records that Jesus' townspeople took offense at Him, asking very cynically where a carpenter could get wisdom and miraculous powers. Jesus said to them, "Only in his hometown and in his own house is a prophet without honor" (Matthew 13:57). Because of their unbelief (rejection), Jesus did not do very many miracles in that place.

Jesus' own people called Him a Samaritan, which was a great insult for Jews in those days, and more than once they said that He had a demon (John 7:20). He was criticized for eating with "unclean" hands (Mark 7:5).

When the religious leaders of the Jews felt they were losing their hold on the people, they began to plot against Jesus. They claimed that He was a blasphemer, because He talked about forgiving sins (Mark 2:6–7). They criticized Him for eating with tax collectors and "sinners"—those who themselves were rejected from society—even though in so doing He brought them salvation (Mark 2:16; Luke 19:7). It must have deeply grieved Jesus that they opposed the work of God that He was doing.

The Pharisees announced that Jesus was possessed by Beelzebub, the prince of demons (Mark 3:22). They tried to test Him by cynically demanding miraculous signs (Mark 8:11–12), challenging His authority (Mark 11:28) and asking difficult questions to try to catch Him unawares (Mark 10:2–12; 12:13–17).

Jesus' trial and death

Jesus repeatedly foretold His coming rejection and death. He said,

> "The Son of Man must suffer many things and be rejected by the elders, chief priests and teachers of the law, and he must be killed."
>
> Luke 9:22

The Son of Man is going to be betrayed into the hands of men.

Luke 9:44

But first he must suffer many things and be rejected by this generation.

Luke 17:25

He will be handed over to the Gentiles. They will mock him, insult him, spit on him, flog him and kill him.

Luke 18:32

Jesus' friends were so slow to understand, but after the resurrection they remembered His words (Luke 24:8).

Many of Jesus' own disciples had already turned back and no longer followed Him because of His "hard teachings." He was betrayed by one of the Twelve, Judas (see Luke 22:3–6, 47–48). When Jesus told the disciples that they would fall away, they refused to believe Him (Matthew 26:35). Peter, although strongly vowing he would never disown Jesus, denied Him three times (Luke 22:34).

At the time of Jesus' great trial in the Garden of Gethsemane, His friends fell asleep. He came to them three times in anguish and found them heavy with sleep each time (Mark 14:37–41). When an armed mob came to arrest Him, everyone deserted Him and fled (Mark 14:42–50).

After Jesus healed on the Sabbath, the Pharisees began to plot with the followers of Herod how they might kill Him (Mark 3:6). The chief priests and the whole Sanhedrin looked for evidence against Him so that they could put Him to death. Many people gave false testimony against Him, although their statements disagreed (Mark 14:55–59).

Jesus suffered unspeakable physical pain as He was being crucified. There was also emotional torment, because He was continually mocked and insulted (Matthew 27:39; Mark 15:31). Yet the spiritual agony of the cross was even greater, because Jesus took our sin on Himself, and that meant abandonment by His own Father.

The rejection of Jesus was made complete when the Father

turned His back on His Son. Jesus cried out, "My God, my God, why have you forsaken me?" (Mark 15:34).

Isaiah wrote,

> He was despised and rejected by men,
>   a man of sorrows, and familiar with suffering.
> Like one from whom men hide their faces,
>   he was despised, and we esteemed him not.
> Surely he took up our infirmities
>   and carried our sorrows,
> yet we considered him stricken by God,
>   smitten by him, and afflicted.
> But he was pierced for our transgressions,
>   he was crushed for our iniquities;
> the punishment that brought us peace was upon him,
>   and by his wounds we are healed . . .
> Yet it was the LORD's will to crush him and cause him to
>   suffer.
>
>   Isaiah 53:3–5, 10

Why? It was all for love. Jesus' death and resurrection became a "divine exchange" for us. He took our rejection. In its place we can receive healing, acceptance, affirmation, love, security and much more.

Study questions:

1. How did Jesus experience rejection in His life on earth?
2. Why did this happen, and what did it have to do with His purpose in coming?
3. How did He respond to the rejection He faced?
4. What did His death on the cross have to do with rejection?
5. How does this affect us and our own experience of rejection?

7

Dealing with Rejection

We have just seen that God has dealt a death blow to rejection through His Son, Jesus. Yet there is a responsibility on our side, too. We cannot be passive: We must take control over areas of rejection in our lives in the power of Jesus' name.

Obadiah prophesied, "On Mount Zion will be deliverance; it will be holy and the house of Jacob will possess its inheritance" (Obadiah 17). We need to take possession of what has been given to us in Christ!

Responsibility

We have a part to play in healing and wholeness. We must answer for our own attitudes and actions, even though the enemy may have gotten in or there is a hereditary factor. As we accept our personal accountability, healing will come within our grasp.

When Jesus began His ministry, He made this great pronouncement: "The Spirit of the Lord is on me, because he has anointed me to preach good news to the poor. He has sent me to proclaim freedom for the prisoners and recovery of sight for the blind, to release the oppressed, and to proclaim the year of the LORD's favor" (Luke 4:18–19). Then He said, "Today this scripture is fulfilled in your hearing" (Luke 4:21). Although this was the prophetic fulfillment of God's will, it nevertheless required Jesus' willing participation. In the same way, we need to exercise our own faith for healing. Revelation demands a response.

The Father heart of God

In the whole area of rejection, it is essential that we recognize and understand the Father's heart. As we have already seen, many people's first experience of rejection is through their earthly parents. Therefore, they may worship God at a distance but feel unable to relate to Him as a loving, caring Father.

The word *Abba* is used three times in the New Testament. As Jesus prayed in the garden of Gethsemane, He called His Father "Abba." This is the same everyday word used in Jewish culture for a child to speak to his daddy. It is a warm and familiar yet respectful term for "father," used also by adult sons and daughters. Yet for Jesus to speak to God in that way was ground-breaking.

This same word is taken up by the Church in Romans 8:15 and Galatians 4:6. We, too, can express our love and requests to the Father by saying to Him, "Abba." We have been adopted into the family of God, and He says to us, "I will be a Father to you, and you will be my sons and daughters" (2 Corinthians 6:18).

God knows that rejection is a barrier between us. As the great Father, His desire is that we have security, peace, emotional stability, affirmation and acceptance. Just as He spoke to Jesus, "You are my Son, whom I love; with you I am well pleased" (Luke 3:21), He also speaks to us.

Our identity is found in relationships. We need to come into a real relationship with God as our Father, receive His acceptance of us and then move into accepting ourselves and others.

But first we have to acknowledge the things that may be barriers.

Disappointment
Disappointment can hinder any response to God's healing presence. Proverbs 13:12 says, "Hope deferred makes the heart sick." When our deep longings for affection and acceptance

have not been met, our frustration and hurt can prevent us from reaching out in faith and trust. This, too, can become a foothold for the enemy.

Shame

The experience of being rejected often leaves a sense of humiliation or shame. The enemy will try to take advantage by accusing us and condemning us, which can easily lead to self-rejection and withdrawal. Yet however painful past events have been, they must be faced with the grace of God. Often as we speak out our confession in the presence of others, the stronghold of shame is broken.

Forgiveness

Whenever there are wounds of rejection, there are people to forgive. We need to look honestly at our feelings toward those who have hurt us, bringing them into the light of God. This may involve confessing our feelings about God. We may well have to forgive ourselves, too.

A parable that Jesus told shows the issue of unforgiveness in a very clear light. A servant who himself had been forgiven a great debt could not forgive others. Therefore, he was sentenced to torment in prison until he paid his own debt (see Matthew 18:21–35). Someone has said, "He that cannot forgive others breaks the bridge over which he must pass himself, for every man has to be forgiven."

We, too, have already been forgiven a debt so big we could never have paid it on our own. The amount far exceeds anything that another person may owe us. In Jesus' story, the master was motivated by mercy and generosity, but his anger flared when he saw the servant's own unwillingness to forgive.

Unforgiveness is sin and will be judged by God, no matter what has happened to us. It imprisons and tortures the one who cannot forgive, and it can create an entrance for demonic powers. It becomes a barrier to our relationship with others and with God.

In Ephesians 2:14, Paul says that Jesus has "destroyed the barrier, the dividing wall of hostility." Through His own body He reconciled us to God and each other. Colossians 2:13–14 tells us that Jesus forgave us all our sins, canceling the written code against us by nailing it on the cross. If a barrier still remains, it is on our side, not God's. And if we refuse to forgive, we are nullifying Jesus' sacrifice.

Forgiveness may need to be a process. How long? We have to keep forgiving until the pain goes. We have to keep forgiving until we begin to see the other person differently, we speak of them and to them differently and we no longer strive to get even. True forgiveness will alter our relationship with the person who has offended us. It will free us to bless and be blessed.

Repentance of sin

Is repentance necessary with rejection? Yes! Rejection is completely bound up with sin. It leads us to sin against ourselves, others and the One who created us. The wrong reactions we have to sins against us can cause us to commit those same sins against others.

We often make repentance too cheap—a quick prayer. Yet it is a costly issue. It is a change of heart, will, thinking and emotions. It is deliberately turning away from sin and turning to God with a change of lifestyle.

Look at the way David repented in Psalm 51. He responded clearly and completely to the Word of God. He fully confessed his own guilt and laid it before God, crying out for forgiveness. Because of this, he was not tormented forever by his sin but was able to make a clean break from it.

Paul gives us a key to repentance in 2 Corinthians 7:8–11. He commends the Corinthians for expressing sorrow that led them to repentance: "Godly sorrow brings repentance that leads to salvation and leaves no regret, but worldly sorrow brings death. See what this godly sorrow has produced in you: what earnestness, what eagerness to clear yourselves, what indignation, what alarm, what longing, what concern, what readiness to see justice done." We need to acknowledge the pain in repentance and also the fact that it takes time, commitment and emotional energy.

In Acts 2:37–38 we read that the people who heard the Word of God were "cut to the heart and said to Peter and the other apostles 'Brothers, what shall we do?' " Peter called them all to repent. We also need to let our hearts be penetrated by the Word of God and respond accordingly. It is then that repentance becomes effective.

Inner healing

Those things that have been fed into our emotional memories do not disappear with time. Negative input will remain to cause us harm unless we can receive inner healing.

Hebrews 13:8 tells us, "Jesus Christ is the same yesterday and today and forever." Jesus is not limited by our time and space. He is outside of it, yet He breaks into it through the Holy Spirit. He is fully capable of healing yesterday's problems and hurts today.

Someone has said, "Inner healing is a ladder, not a single rung; a process, rarely a one-time event." Those of us who counsel and pray for healing must bear that in mind. In the pressure to get things sorted out, it is easy to be insensitive. It may be good to prepare for a time of ministry by fasting or reading specific Scriptures.

In inner healing, we need to acknowledge the hurts and wounded memories and surrender them to Jesus, asking the Holy Spirit to bring healing. We must allow a release of emotion—we must let it happen and not push the feelings of pain down.

In the case of rejection, deliverance is often needed along with inner healing. The ability to distinguish between spirits is a gift of the Holy Spirit (1 Corinthians 12:10). We need to be able to discern what is from God, what is from ourselves and what is demonic—sometimes it is not easy!

If you are certain that there is some demonic intrusion, take authority in prayer and cast out the demon, being as specific as possible. If there is a struggle with a manifestation of some kind, press through. There may need to be more than one session. Finally, ask the Holy Spirit to fill the empty place with God's presence (see Luke 11:14–26).

Finally, broken relationships can be restored. Because we have been reconciled to God through the cross, we can be reconciled to each other. In place of enmity there can be friendship. As deep wounds are healed, trust can be restored, and the peace of God can rule again in place of fear.

As we come out of rejection, breaking the bread of Holy Communion can be an appropriate response. Jesus said, "Do this in remembrance of me." Our newfound acceptance can be considered in the light of the cross. Jesus died and then rose from the dead so that we could live in freedom and relationship with God. Identity, security and esteem are all part of what we receive from Jesus' broken body.

Study questions:

1. What responsibility do we have as Christians for our own healing and wholeness?
2. What is the Father heart of God, and what does it have to do with rejection?
3. In what way is forgiveness important?
4. Why do people suffering from rejection need to repent?
5. How does inner healing come about?

8

Moving On from Rejection

Who would have chosen a failure like Peter to preach on the Day of Pentecost? After vowing never to leave Jesus, he deserted Him with oaths and curses. No wonder he went away weeping bitterly (see Luke 22:54–62). He returned to his old job, no longer considered one of the disciples.

Yet Jesus appeared at the lakeside and confronted Peter, challenging him three times—once for every time Peter had denied Him (see John 21:15–19). Through this persistence, Peter's identity, direction and role were restored. He was healed of the past and given purpose for the future.

Many of us can identify with Peter's sense of failure and self-rejection. We need the restoration he received, as well as the discipling that came with it.

It is important that pastoral care follows prayer for deliverance and healing. After deep ministry, it may not be easy for people to carry on in isolation. The Church needs to disciple believers, and those who have received prayer must be willing to be discipled. By practicing these basic disciplines of the faith, we can grow out of rejection and into maturity.

Maintaining healing

After a time of prayer, it is necessary to press forward in healing. We all need good, honest relationships in which it is possible to talk and pray things through on an ongoing basis. Some people feel disoriented for a while after prayer for healing and deliverance. Good and consistent communication is important for accountability. Therefore, it is helpful to plan times to assess progress. If the person who originally prayed is not able to continue contact, find someone else in the local church to do follow-up. In this way, the growth and healing can continue.

The following areas of discipleship must all be considered.

1. **Spiritual knowledge:** Understanding of the power of the cross and the crucified life is vital in the ongoing warfare with the flesh and demonic powers.

2. **Scripture:** Reading, applying and living from the Word of God is essential to keeping our freedom in Jesus.

3. **Prayer and praise:** Thanking and worshiping God for His work of release is part of the process of growth.

4. **Renewing the mind:** Exercising self-control in the area of emotions, thoughts, and will is important to prevent further attacks from the enemy.

5. **Positive confession:** First Corinthians 14:3 tells us to strengthen, encourage and build up one another with our speech.

6. **The Father heart of God:** Each person must learn to relate to God as a loving Father.

7. **Healthy sexuality:** Often there are identity issues to do with masculinity and femininity that must be worked out.

8. **Confidence and self-esteem:** Self-worth and value that have been undermined by rejection must be restored.

9. **The Body of Christ:** Both giving and receiving in the local church is part of growth and maturity.

10. **Submission and resisting:** James 4:7 tells us to resist the enemy and submit to God—relating rightly to authority.

11. **Laughter:** Nehemiah 8:10 tells us that the joy of the Lord is our strength!

As we trust the Holy Spirit to guide us, and trust others to support us, we will grow in our walk with Jesus. We must learn to live in the opposite spirit to rejection. Yes, there will be failure, but in Christ we can learn to overcome. God wants all of His children to know His acceptance, forgiveness, affirmation and blessing.

Study questions:

1. What does the story of Peter's restoration teach us about how Jesus ministered inner healing?
2. In what way should the Church help those who have received deliverance and prayer for healing?
3. What does it mean to disciple believers?
4. Name some important areas of discipleship.
5. In what way can we personally go on being healed?

Appendix

Family History Questionnaire

In counseling, I have found it very helpful to ask a series of questions relating to the counselee's history. The object is to look at the person's history from conception right through to where he or she is today.

This method saves time while clearly pinpointing specific issues for follow-up. I often give out the questionnaire a week or two in advance, which allows time for the questions to be answered honestly and thoughtfully.

Going through these questions will open up issues of a person's life that will be important in his or her healing. We need to do this in an atmosphere of prayer, and trust the Holy Spirit to bring the most pertinent issues to the forefront.

1. What is your first memory?

2. Were you wanted?

3. Were you illegitimate?

4. Was there an attempted abortion?

5. Did your birth follow a miscarriage or stillbirth?

6. Did your parents want a child of a different sex?

7. Was the birth traumatic?

8. Were you and your mother able to bond together?

9. Who brought you up?

10. How well do you know your father?

11. Was he away much during your childhood?

12. Did you receive affectionate hugs and kisses from your parents?

13. Who disciplined you and how?

14. Did your parents take time to listen to you?

15. Can you remember either of your parents turning away when you needed help?

16. How did you try to get attention from your parents?

17. What is your most unhappy memory?

18. Who was the dominant force in your home?

19. Was anyone "always right" in your family?

20. How did your parents relate to each other?

21. Are your parents still together, and how do they relate now?

22. If there was separation or divorce, what do you remember about it?

23. Whose lap would you sit on?

24. What was your order of birth?

25. Were there favorites in your family?

26. Did you relate well to your brothers/sisters?

27. Did you like school? What are your memories?

28. Did you go to a boarding school? At what age?

29. Was there legalism or religious pressure in your home?

30. Can you remember any negative words that were applied to you?

31. Do you like yourself?

32. Do you dislike or feel threatened by men?

33. Do you dislike or feel threatened by women?

34. Do you eat regularly? Were there unusual eating habits in your family

35. Have you ever thought about suicide?

36. Do you have troubled sleep or nightmares? What are they?

37. Do you have sexual difficulties or a troubled thought life?

38. How did you learn about sex, and from whom?

39. Have you engaged in sex outside of marriage?

40. Was there any inappropriate sexual attention or abuse while you were growing up?

41. Did you experience any physical or mental abuse?

42. Do you have strange feelings toward people of the same sex?

43. Have you been used for lust (money, sex, power) rather than loved for yourself?

44. Do you struggle with feelings of shame?

45. Do you struggle with guilty feelings? If so, what for?

46. Have you experienced great disappointment or been let down and betrayed?

47. Is there anyone you have difficulty forgiving?

48. Do you have any habits you cannot control?

49. Are you afraid of anyone or anything?

50. If you are married, have you felt dominated by your partner?

51. Have you experienced separation or divorce?

52. Do you feel used and abused in your marriage?

53. Are you a single parent? Has that led to hurt and rejection?

54. Do you feel discarded by the Church or have difficulty making relationships in the Church?

55. How do you relate to authority figures, including church leaders?

56. Have you been unemployed?

57. Have you experienced rejection in your workplace or in applying for jobs?

58. Is there any freemasonry in your family or ancestry?

59. Is there any family involvement in superstition, spiritism, séances, magic, ~~faith healing~~, tarot cards, ouija boards or other occult practices?

60. Have you been hypnotized?

61. Have you been involved in any of the martial arts, yoga, or transcendental meditation (TM)?

62. Do you feel you have failed God?

63. Do you long for affection and love?

64. Do you find it hard to express emotions? What happens to them?

65. Do your emotions come out in an explosion, or do they hurt you inside?

66. Do you weep very much? Are there particular reasons why?

67. Do you find it difficult to communicate what you are thinking and feeling?

68. What kind of a relationship do you have with your own children?

69. Do you find it difficult to affirm your children?

70. Do you frequently criticize your children?

71. Do you love your family with actions or words?

72. Do you know God's affirmation, or do you hear, "Do more"?

73. Do you say positive things to other people?

74. Do you say what other people want to hear in order to please them?

75. Do you feel the need to justify yourself or defend yourself from attack?

76. Do you have difficulty trusting people? Are you afraid of being taken advantage of?

77. Do you find it difficult to apologize when you have done something wrong?
78. Do you think that if people knew your failings they would reject or abandon you?
79. Has God ever said to you, "You're forgiven"?
80. Is God your "Abba"?

Steve Hepden has been in full-time Christian work since 1981. His church leadership experience includes pastoring, preaching, teaching and planting new works. Over the years Steve has become well known, both nationally and internationally, as a gifted teacher with a powerful prophetic edge. He is also a popular conference speaker.

Steve ministers on a wide range of subjects, but his overriding passion is for people to come into wholeness, spirit, soul and body, and to live an "authentic" Christian life, possessing all that God has for them. He has a particular ministry to those who suffer from rejection and a poor self-image.

Along with his wife, Chris, Steve is also the author of *What Christians Should Know about Their Value to God*. He is currently studying for a masters degree in applied theology. He and Chris live in northwest England.